Every 30 seconds another person becomes a victim of human trafficking.[1]

---

[1] "Human Trafficking—the Problem," Call to Freedom, accessed June 7, 2018. http://calltofreedom.org/human-trafficking/

Over twenty-five years ago, my life was altered. There are so many words that could describe the events—but the word "altered" fits best. It all began from a divinely set up flight delay which caused my husband, Rusty, to run into Philip Cameron in an airport. I say it was divine because when God is ready to move and shift and bring people together, to make something happen, He will go to great lengths to speak to people, trusting in their obedience for His will to take place. Philip gave Rusty a VHS tape and shared with him the horrors of what was taking place in the country of Moldova. Rusty knew he needed to get the tape to our pastor, and when he did, our church sowed a seed—and God's timetable began. Little did we know this was just the beginning of continued sowing, going, building, believing, loving, and committing to this ministry, and the girls and boys who were about to walk into our hearts.

For all these years, we have had the privilege of meeting and being deeply involved in the lives of many of the girls and boys. Their stories have moved us to tears and provoked us to act—but what I have witnessed over the past five years goes beyond the devastation of what their beginnings would dictate their end to be. Instead, I have witnessed firsthand how God can truly redeem and give back beauty for ashes...when you give Him the ashes.

God began the process over twenty-five years ago when He set up that chance meeting between Philip and Rusty. He had "heard the cry of the orphan" (Exodus 22:23), and He was responding. As Philip says, He threw a long ball, knowing the timing of when churches across America would say, "Yes," catching that ball at just the right time so that Dasa and all the others would feel the full impact of His love, His purpose, and His destiny on their lives. There was no greater moment than the day I watched Dasa and the others stand up in the orphanage they grew up in and give hope and a future to girls who had been just like them. I have watched firsthand as they have embraced the pain, rejection, disappointment, and abandonment, giving it back to Jesus, and in turn watching Him making "all things new." I have witnessed the girls coming full-circle and the hand of God using them to now carry the same message into the same places, where they were lost and then found. Their purpose has been fueled by the passion to see the lost saved, the broken healed, and the endangered rescued. Their stories are kissed by Heaven because in His kingdom, when sons and daughters are born, they are heirs. And these—have the attention of heaven.

-Pastor Leisa L. Nelson
The Rock Family Worship Center

In the world today, many people are imprisoned by their story. For my friend Dasa it is the opposite. Her own story has proven to open prison doors, for she now lives in freedom. Her ability to write and bring the truth of the story to erase the pain of the prison is phenomenal. This book shows how a life can be taken away in 30 seconds by human trafficking. Dasa has become the voice for so many young people who have no one to tell their story. Thank God for an author who became the voice for those who were not heard.

-Lloyd Zeigler
CEO Masters Commission International Network

EVERY 30 SECONDS

Compiled by Dasa Rosca

Every 30 Seconds

Compiled by Dasa Rosca

Published by The Orphan's Hands

P.O. Box 242248

Montgomery, Alabama 36124

(334) 456-5544

www.theorphanshands.org

This book or parts thereof may not be reproduced in any form, stored in a retrieval system, or transmitted in any form by any means—electronic, mechanical, photocopy, recording, or otherwise—without prior written permission of the publisher, except as provided by United States of America copyright law.

Copyright ©2018 by Philip Cameron

All rights reserved

ISBN Paperback: 978-0-692-14859-4

Printed in the United States of America

To you,
may your story not be forgotten.

CONTENTS

Foreword 1

Introduction 13

Olga 17

Luiza 25

Natalia 31

Anetilia 37

Catea 43

Alina 47

Oxana 51

Liviu 57

Tudor 65

Nicolae 71

Afterthought 74

Human Trafficking Statistics 81

What You Can Do 85

Foreword

After learning that suffering and adversity builds a platform for deeper connections with God, others, and ourselves, Jazgul Orozova grabbed a pen and started writing about it. She has blended her passion for God, "the least of these," and books and turned them into writing pieces. She writes as a form of prayer and as therapy for her experiences growing up in an orphanage.

Jazgul was born in Kyrgyzstan and raised in an orphanage in Moldova. She is currently living in Nashville, Tennessee, where she attends Lipscomb University. Jazgul has worked with Missions Without Borders, World Team, Charity Cup, and Justice and Mercy International mentoring and helping underprivileged children and orphans in Moldova.

Today she is a member of UNICEF USA Congregational Actions Team, where she advocates for the protection of children's rights, which has enabled her, along with other students, to launch UNICEF on campus at Lipscomb University. This poem is a glimpse into her life and her vulnerability, which she believes is what makes her strong.

Words Are Medicine

Here is how it works: You find a room where you can be by yourself so you can avoid giving anyone a reason to call you crazy.

You take a piece of paper or your computer with you.

You open a blank page and start bleeding into it.

For the next few hours, you don't think words.

You feel them.

Foreword

You don't stop.

You laugh, cry, and have a drink to help you numb the pain.

You write in English, even if it's broken English.

The words weigh less in your third language.

They seem to hurt less.

You write, about your childhood in the orphanage.

About how you found out you have a little sister and then an older one, who became eternal before you became human.

You write,

About all the trails of blood, you left behind

And how you had to fight like hell to keep yourself alive.

Because this world was everything else but kind

To your soul.

You write,

About how you had to be tough to protect and shield yourself;

You write,

How you painted your fears into the color of your eyes

So no one would notice them.

You write,

About your parents and what it is like to live in their absence.

You wonder, how can someone bring life and not want to keep it?

You wonder, if you ever disappear, would anyone notice?

You see parents holding their children and you smile

Knowing that your biggest dream, for them is a reality

You write,

How you learned to be your own mother and father.

You write,

Foreword

About forgiveness along with the stories of those who drained you of your worth,

About the times you craved revenge.

How you wished every breath your father would take in,

Would hurt him as much as your breath did.

If he wasn't breathing, you wished his grave would never grow flowers on it.

And every time you'd hear his name,

You'd shrink

Because all he gave you was shame

And the blood that runs through your veins

You never wanted it.

You write,

How you realize you want to know what forgiveness tastes like

You tell yourself, "He is behind."

Keeping him inside of you will intoxicate your mind

And soul

Forgive.

You repeat, "Forgive,"

Until it becomes your daily mana you feed yourself with

To keep on going

You remind yourself that your life is worth so much more

Than your mom wanted to sell it for

In a train station

You write,

About all your tattoos, the stories you wear on your body

The ones you never wanted exposed

Because you were afraid of the pointing fingers of this world.

You write,

About your best friend you met in the orphanage and how she would share her two pieces of bread

And every night would hug you tight

Foreword

Like she was afraid

There would be no tomorrow.

You write,

How she'd steal apples so you could quiet your stomach.

You write,

How she would make you smile ear to ear and soften your heart

And remind you that life is a piece of art

We can paint on,

With colors, we want.

You feel your pain diminishing and you keep on writing.

You write,

About how you survived cold winter, barefooted and hungry.

How you bloomed again, just like snow-drops pushing right up through the cold.

You write,

How you learned to love this life

With all its limitations and triumphs.

How you learned to look for reasons to laugh and realized that life offers many reasons to do so.

You write, how you learned to dream again.

Then you stop.

You look at what you've written and you think it's stupid, messy, and it has too much dirt on it.

But the dirtier the page is, the cleaner and lighter your heart feels.

So you push on.

You know you must uncover the wounds so you can sew yourself back together. But. God. It. Hurts.

It hurts like a bunch of needles constantly piercing through your body

You think: "Life is not an easy place to be in."

"It is ugly."

You also think how beautiful it is.

Foreword

The laughter, the love, the people, the sunrise, the ocean, the mountains, the breeze, the morning dew...

You know life is not either.

Life is both.

And you write that down too.

You write,

About all those times you begged God to do something and He didn't.

How you raged against Him, how you cursed and pointed your finger at Him.

Then you go on about how you realized there is no one left but HIM and you decided to give that guy another try.

You close your eyes

Let Him do the talking.

He answers, telling you things which make no sense to you.

Somehow you are okay with that.

It's the peace and comfort that keeps you wanting more,

And His presence doesn't make your heart less sore,

It just gives you hope and meaning.

His words slowly become music to your soul, the kind you want to play over and over.

You feel Him opening His palms and showing you His scars.

You open your heart and you show Him yours.

You feel like He understands.

He tells you that there are other layers to your suffering, like meaning and purpose.

You take that and go to see those whose fears you understand.

You go back to the orphanage, to visit those you see yourself in.

You dance, laugh, and pray with them.

You spend countless hours feeling alive.

You hug them tight

They hug you tighter,

You wipe their tears

They wipe yours,

Then you cry harder.

In the moments like this, many of your "whys" have been answered

You see Jesus smiling at you and you smile back.

You sit for hours listening to their stories

You write those stories among yours.

You feel waves of joy.

You look at the time and you realize you have been there for five hours.

You look at what you have created, you save it and store it in a folder no one would find.

You take air in,

You exhale deeply

You feel your heart growing bigger.

You feel the relief from the deep marrow of your bones

You see how your pain is leading you to create beauty

You feel alive.

Stronger.

Fresher.

Braver.

Next time you go to see your therapist and she asks you how you are

You smile and say, "I am doing great; I'm taking my medicine."

Jazgul Orozova

Introduction

It was almost thirty years ago when Philip Cameron heard about orphans living in terrible conditions in Romania. He went there for what he thought was one visit. What he saw and what he felt changed his life forever.

Philip was a successful minister in America. He was an author, recording artist, TV personality. When he saw the conditions children were living in, he changed his life to help those who had no hope.

Philip and his wife, Chrissie, adopted a child from an orphanage in Timisoara, Romania. As the little boy Andrew grew, they were compelled to return repeatedly to his orphanage to help. New toilets, beds, roof, were all given to help the two hundred children Philip and Chrissie couldn't adopt.

Twenty years ago, they began going to Moldova. Since then they have been involved in rebuilding orphanages and building homes for young people at risk. Philip's motto, "If you are born, God has a plan," is the driving force behind all that he and his family have done over the last thirty years. The Orphan's Hands ministry is the result of their faith and hard work.

This book will give you a glimpse into the lives of young men and women who started out in life as a statistic. Today, every 30 seconds another person becomes a victim of human trafficking.[2] Slavery has never been a thing of the past, and sadly, these lives left unprotected become the main source for human traffickers. The Orphan's Hands provides them with a safe home and a means to an education, which prevents these vulnerable kids from ending up in

---

[2] "Human Trafficking— The Problem," Call to Freedom.

Introduction

human bondage. With the support of the people who cared deeply and of course their own personal willingness to give themselves a chance, they have overcome against all odds. Today they are success stories with a compassion for the world that is deeply rooted in their souls and manifesting in their daily life.

Every word you will read in this book is a torn puzzle piece from their past, their present, and most importantly their hope for the future. Once you read these stories you will hopefully realize that unless you stand up for the least of these and protect them, their lives will have a terrifying end. I encourage you to see the need to break the circle of victimization and partner with The Orphan's Hands that will cast a light on human trafficking and stop the madness of modern-day slavery.

Dasa Rosca

Olga

The final dark hours before the sun brought the light were always the hardest. A new day never meant hope for me. It only meant the mess my life was in would continue before I had a chance to process another day that was now gone. It is rough to remember the painful state I was in when I was growing up in a small village in the Ukraine. I know people say that it never rains forever, but when I look back at my life, all I can see is a never-ending storm.

My father, who was born into a family of alcoholics, became the only thing he thought he knew how to be: an alcoholic himself. By the time I was born, there was nothing left of him or his life. Growing up

I wished it could have all been different. I wished I could have been the reason for him to break the cycle and not let history repeat itself. He never felt any sense of responsibility for me. I have always felt betrayed by him for letting alcohol take such a strong hold of him and his world.

Unlike my father, my mother's reason for quitting on the family was that she was mentally unstable. This is the excuse my grandparents gave me, at least. When I was only six months old, my mother started having affairs, and I was left in the care of my alcoholic and absent father. When I was three, a woman found me walking alone through the village and took me to my grandparents' house, where I lived for the next few years. Life became somewhat better with them. They were the only people who made me believe that someday everything would make perfect sense and that life had meaning.

When I first found out I had a sister, I was hurt by the thought that my mother would bring another child into the world. She had given up on me not too long before, and here she was now dropping off another baby girl, Angelina. But with time, my sister's presence started to comfort me. Often, I was so focused on her that I would forget about my own heartache. Unfortunately, our somewhat normal life didn't last long.

My mother stormed back into our life. She, like most people of her kind, made countless promises with no intention to keep them, and just like that, we were now living with her and her new husband. The physical and verbal abuse began right away. Today I sit and contemplate just how broken you would have to be inside that you would wish for your own mother to abandon you once more. I know I was shattered. There were not broken pieces; there was only dust.

All I wanted at that time was for my mother to quit on me one more time.

My stepfather's favorite form of punishment was to make me kneel on hard dried corn. I did that. Not once or twice, but countless times. My stepfather was a drunk just like my own father had been. There was no escape from him after a few glasses of vodka. This time around, though, my mother was actually there, and every night once his friends left, he came for me, my sister, and my mother, and we got what he said we deserved. The walls of our house were splattered with my mother's blood, and still she didn't want to leave him. Some of the hardest moments that felt like an eternity were the nights my little sister cried in her crib from starvation. Our bedroom was taken over by rats, and I was just too little and too scared to walk over to her. I have never felt as helpless as I felt during those nights. My days were spent knocking at people's doors to buy wine for my stepfather and his friends. I also begged them for food for my little sister and me. Somehow there was always enough money for the wine, but never for our food.

We were very weak when grandma finally took us away from them. Because of our grandparents, we survived. They cared for us day and night until grandma got ill and life once again changed. My little sister, Angelina, was only two years old when a Christian family from the village took her to live with them. I was hurt and disappointed my grandparents let go of her. I was simply too young to understand that they were only trying to give her a better chance in life. Living with my grandparents was great. They fed me, clothed me, and took me to church every Sunday. They worked hard to make my life a little easier, and I will forever be grateful to have had them in my life.

A few years later my mother gave birth to my little brother, Alex. It was no surprise when she showed up at my grandparent's house with him and left without him. Alex was also adopted by the same family that had adopted my little sister Angelina. It was his only chance at survival, and this time around I understood that. I had the opportunity to grow up in the same village as them and see them as often as I wanted to. Our mother only showed up when she needed food. I can still see her filling her bags with food, closing the door behind her, and walking away from me.

Now that I am older I understand more. I have struggled to accept the things I cannot change. I have worked hard to focus on the good things I was given in life: my grandparents, who I will forever be thankful for, and now the ministry that has made it possible for me to have a future. I was raised knowing about God's love for me, but today I actually feel His love. I am no longer helpless or hopeless.

Luiza

The ones with a story like mine will know what I mean when I say I lived my whole life with a tight grip on my heart. I think one of the hardest things you will ever have to do in life is learn to accept that what your parents have done had nothing to do with you. I grew up believing they gave up on me because I wasn't worth their time. I couldn't silence this powerful thought that stopped me from processing life as it was, until one day I realized I was grieving over people who were still alive.

My mother was only seventeen years old when she gave birth to me. Of course, there have been countless days I wish she hadn't, but she did. My father, who I guess was just as young as she was, took off as soon as he heard about me. Growing up, whenever the storm inside of me got to be too much to handle, I would imagine the one moment that could have changed everything. I found peace in the thought that if my father had taken one look at me, he never would have left. I will never know if there is any truth to that. The more time went by, the better I learned to control these raw feelings. It wasn't a strategy; it was survival plain and simple.

The sad part is that my mother did look into my eyes when she gave birth to me and yet she still abandoned me shortly after. She had her whole life ahead of her, and I wasn't going to be the reason why she couldn't live it. It was my grandfather who took me in and cared for me until the day he passed away. I was his life, and he was both a mother and a father to me.

With his death, my mother had no other choice but to take me to live with her. At the time she was sharing her life with an abusive man. Shortly after I went to live with them my mother gave birth to a boy, Colea. I remember watching her caring for him and growing more resentful by the day. I couldn't grasp the thought that she loved him and not me.

Everything changed once again the day my stepfather was sentenced to prison for murder. I watched my mother as she stopped loving my baby brother and started loving the bottle of vodka. It didn't take long before she brought home another man. My second brother, Andrei, was born and brought into a home full of empty vodka bottles and nonstop swearing. There was no love and care this time around. It was pure negligence. My mother and her drinking buddy would disappear for days at a time, leaving me to care for myself and my younger brothers. I stopped attending school in order to do that.

It was a teacher who reported my mother to social services after finding my brothers and me home alone one day. My brother Colea and I were immediately taken away and placed in an orphanage. Our situation didn't improve. In fact, the living conditions at the orphanage were much worse than at home. Most of my days were spent making up excuses for the fact that our mother didn't come to fight to get us back. The day I was taken to the orphanage was the last time I saw my mother. Her last words to me were that I was the reason her life was ruined. With time she turned from someone I loved into someone I hated.

When we got older we were moved to a different orphanage. It was a Christian orphanage—very different from everything I had experienced in my life. It took me a while to understand why so many abandoned children stuck in an orphanage were full of joy. It was because they had a different source of joy than what our life had been offering to us so far. They had God.

The day my brothers and I left this orphanage to go live with a Christian foster family was an act of His love toward us. We were loved and cared for by this family like we had never been before. It was a time when we thought our life was only going to get better from that point on. But the conflict between the Ukraine and Russia took that chance away from us. The village we were living in was under the control of the Russian military forces. The roads got destroyed by explosives. The school got closed down. We had no electricity, no water, and no heating. Once again, I became uncertain of my future.

Thankfully, God was watching out for me. It was an early morning in June when a team from The Orphan's Hands reached our village after driving for eleven hours. They were there to deliver groceries and clothing to the families in the village that were struggling the most. The Orphan's Hands also delivered hope for me that day. I am now in a safe home, away from the conflict zone. A home where His love is always present, and a future is made possible through the work of The Orphan's Hands. My story is mostly made up of a collection of sorrowful moments, until the day I learned about His love for me. I no longer have that tight grip on my heart, because now He has a tight grip on my life.

Natalia

In my life one thing is for certain: my strength came from knowing weakness. My story began like most of the stories in this book. I was born into a family not only stricken by poverty but also by disease. I had no notion of dreams and hopes. There was pain and there was hard work. For my mother's sake and mine, I understood that I couldn't stay a captive of my temporary circumstances. I worked hard, and I patiently waited for a better tomorrow.

I must say that there were many moments when I wondered if my father had been alive if things would have been different. I was only six years old when he passed away. With his death, the misery of our situation truly began. First, my two older brothers, Valeriu and Serghei, who are physically disabled, were placed in an orphanage for children with disabilities where they spent fourteen years. Today they are living in a community home for disabled people somewhere near our village. This was definitely something I didn't understand or accept in the beginning. I watched my mother trying to hide her concern for them over the years, ignoring her own suffering when thinking of them. Now when I look back at our life I am content knowing that they were spared of all those cold nights and the starvation my mother and I suffered for so long.

Since I can remember, my mother has suffered from rheumatoid arthritis. The more time went by, the more the disease took over her body and her mind. At one point she just gave up on everything and started spending most of her time in bed. When I think of my mother, I think of all the times I lay awake next to her trying to calm her pain, trying to help her get through the night.

I believe the only reason I was still at home with her was because physically I was in better shape than my brothers were. Later, I was also diagnosed with dysplastic coxarthrosis. Even though this came with a new set of challenges, most days I was so focused on my mother's pain and suffering that I forgot about my own. My mother's disability pension wasn't enough to cover our expenses, and most of the time we had to choose between pain medication, food, or firewood for the winter. I often went to bed hungry and in pain. Most nights I held my mother's hand through her pain while also hoping we wouldn't freeze to death in our house. Despite my own disability, I carried on.

It was a cold winter day. I came home from school and walked in to see a group of strangers gathered around my mother's bed. She wasn't smiling. The pain she had endured for decades has taken that possibility away from her. In fact, she looked confused and somewhat sadder than usual. I introduced myself to everyone and leaned against the wall on the right side of my mother's bed. On the edge of the bed I noticed a cardboard box with a round sticker on it that read: The Orphan's Hands. It was a care package—a care package that has changed my life. That was the better tomorrow I patiently waited on for all those years. My mother and I had a huge feast that night and plenty of food left to get us through for a while. That night was the first night in my life I went to bed with not just a full belly, but also a future full of hope. I lay awake for hours afraid to fall asleep and wake up from this dream.

High school graduation was only a few months away, something I wasn't looking forward to. I had worked so hard in school. I wanted to make my mother proud, and she was every single time I made the honor roll. My good grades were always the thing that made her smile, and I wasn't ready for that to end.

Only a few short months after that cold winter day, I got accepted and was given a full scholarship at the College of Medicine.

A care package brought hope into my life, and the group of strangers that brought it soon became my family. The Orphan's Hands has given me the safety of a home and an opportunity for an education, something I never thought I would have. I no longer go to bed hungry and in pain. They have given me the opportunity to wake up every morning and work on my dream to become a doctor. My and my mother's future has completely changed because of a care package that reached a village north of Moldova on a cold winter day.

I can't tell if it was my own pain or the depth of my mother's pain that led to the choices I made and respect to this day. The choice to work hard in school and carry on despite everything that was happening in my life. My better tomorrow came with the promise that God sure knows what He is doing, and it came in a cardboard box. Just because the beginning of your life is a little harsh, don't lose hope. Work hard and be patient, and greater things will come into existence. He has a plan.

Anetilia

Deep inside is where the damage hides. You might never get to see the bruises we wear, but trust me, they are there. There was a time when deep inside nothing was fine, and every fall I survived left me crippled a little more than the one before.

There might not be a future when you're poor, but there is always a past. Both of my parents grew up in horrendous poverty, and in poverty they gave birth to my sister and me. I was only two years old when my father left for Russia with the promise to find a job, so he could provide for us. This is something completely normal in Moldova. Parents always make a promise and then they leave. Most of them start a new family wherever they go and stop claiming the one they left behind. My father did just that. We got a phone call from him one day letting us know that he wouldn't be coming back and asking us to get out of his house because he needed money and wanted to sell it. That is when my childhood turned into a wish to simply vanish.

As soon as we moved out of the house my mother began working at a nightclub. She would leave me and my sister home alone and would be gone until the early hours of the morning. I fell asleep at night holding on to the idea that at least I had my mother and that when I woke up in the morning, she would still be there. Time changed that though. She became more distant and stopped coming straight home after work. The times she did make it home, it felt like it was just a rest stop for her, not for the small family that needed her to survive. It wasn't long before my sister chose the same lifestyle as my mother, and then I found myself completely abandoned.

It's never the feeling of hunger, the cold nights of winter, or the dirty clothes you wore that stay with you. With time those feelings detach themselves from you and become isolated flashbacks. The undeniable scraps of my past will always be the stares of disgust from people and the pointing of fingers, like somehow I had control over my family's poor decisions in life.

The day my mother left for Russia, my life crumbled completely. To this day, I don't know how those like me are expected ever to be normal, to build a successful life when all you have is a collapsed foundation. All I felt like doing then was screaming, "Cruel life, please stop shaking me. My foundation is already gone." Yes, I was furious at everyone and everything.

The next few days were spent on the streets. I begged, I cried, I felt absolute fear. It was my sister's alcoholic boyfriend who took us in, and only because my sister was already pregnant with his child. Until my sister gave birth I was nothing but an extra load to them. Then, I became the nanny. My sister and her boyfriend went back to clubs, drinking and fighting nonstop. I spent my time caring for her child and wishing I could disappear. It was as simple as believing that I had nothing to offer the world and the world had nothing to offer me except the torment it already had.

I found out about The Orphan's Hands through a Christian center. After years of abandonment and abuse, I finally arrived home and had the blessing of a huge family that came with it. I no longer had to worry about food, clothes, and a bed to sleep in. They didn't see my past, they saw my future, and that meant the world to me. It meant that I was given the chance to rebuild the foundation that had crumbled under my parents' mistakes over the years. It meant that to God there is no inside damage that He cannot repair.

Catea

I have always believed that compassion makes a person beautiful. When someone's life has been nothing but an obstacle course and somehow that person manages to come out on the other end filled with goodness and compassion instead of bitterness, well, to me, that is simply admirable. It is important not to let what happens on the outside dictate how you feel on the inside.

Shortly after I was born, my parents lost the house they owned, on a technicality. We ended up on the street. Neither of my parents had a stable job, and it wasn't long before my father began to find his comfort in alcohol. Fortunately, my grandmother who owned a two-bedroom shed felt sorry for us and took us in. Our life with her was no better than the life we had on the street. There was no heating system and no indoor plumbing. The two bedrooms were shared between ten people. The adults were so obsessed about their only joy in life, alcohol, that they often forgot to feed us. We barely stayed alive in those conditions.

I was three years old when my parents took me and my older sister, Angela, to the orphanage. I was too young to remember now what I thought the moment they walked away from us. I imagine I must have been confused and maybe afraid that night and the many nights that followed. Because of the age difference, my sister and I got separated. Now I understand that we had different paths to follow, but at three years old I couldn't possibly grasp my situation.

Life at the orphanage wasn't easy. It got worse when I grew older and began to understand more and feel the consequences of being left behind by my parents. I could never count on the teachers; they always gave me the impression that they were only there as long as they were getting paid. I wasn't worth their time, in fact, none of the children were.

My parents never came to visit once during those twelve long years I spent at the orphanage. When I saw them during school breaks, which is the only time the government requires the parents to take their children home in order to save money, I begged for them to keep me instead of sending me back. I wished for them to love me, to want me, and to protect me. But as soon as the school break was over my sister and I were sent back to the orphanage. I realized that I couldn't count on my parents to be there for us no matter how much I wished for that.

I was sixteen years old when my journey at the orphanage came to an end. Believe it or not, it was a sad day. It was my only home for so long. I was heartbroken because all I kept thinking about was that there was no way forward for me. There was no life worth living outside the orphanage. Well, I was wrong.

Through my older sister, Angela, I met the Cameron family. I was welcomed into the huge and amazing family of The Orphan's Hands. For the first time in my life, I was loved, wanted, and accepted. I have hope for my future. Everyone should know that the obstacles in life will come and go, but what will remain are the lessons you have learned from them. Let these lessons make you compassionate.

Alina

Looking back at the mess my life used to be, I wish to change nothing except the moment I gave up on myself. But now that I know what giving up feels like, I can make sure never to quit again, no matter how much I stumble along the way.

The earliest childhood memory I have is of my parents fighting. Early in the morning, in the middle of the day, or most often late at night, they argued. The day they decided to give up on each other they also gave up on me completely. My mother moved to another country, and my father started a family with a different woman. I was abandoned by both and ended up living with my grandparents.

I spent my time trying to understand the reasons why I wasn't wanted. My grandparents spent their time struggling to feed me, clothe me, and put me through school. I told myself every day that today was going to be the day my parents would walk through the blue metal gate right back into my life. I waited until the day I was old enough to walk out through the gate on my own.

The most painful moment in my entire life was when I knocked on my father's door and begged him to allow me to stay. Even though my father did open the door to his home for me then, he never managed to open his heart to me. He spent his days looking for reasons to get rid of me. One day he simply told me that I wasn't his daughter and that he wanted nothing to do with me. Defeated, I found my way back to my grandmother's house.

All I knew at that time was that I wasn't wanted. I simply had no hope and no will to keep on living the life that made no sense to me at all. I told myself that the struggle wasn't worth it. These ideas took over my mind and brought me to the lowest point in my life. I felt empty to the point that one day I tried to commit suicide by cutting my veins.

Alina

I didn't believe in miracles until the moment I regained consciousness at the hospital. I was found by my best friend, who called an ambulance, which ultimately saved my life. Once I got better I began going to the local church in the village. With time, I learned that there is a God. I realized that I couldn't find my place on earth because our time here is only a temporary visit and heaven is our destination.

Today I am thankful for so many things in my life, but most of all I am thankful to God for giving me a second chance. I now know that there is a reason for every struggle. God has a plan even when we believe that letting go of ourselves is the only way out. God is constant! I am beyond grateful to The Orphan's Hands for being the spark of hope when I needed it most. We stumble and we fall, but with His help we get up again, and if we dare to look back we will see a road full of imperfect miracles that led to one perfect message.

Oxana

It doesn't matter how much time goes by or how well you've managed to do after all you went through in life. One question will always haunt you. Why me? Yes, you do survive the mess and you somehow manage to preserve some shred of goodness and kindness, but you also get to spend the rest of your life wondering why others had it easier than you.

I was only five months old when I lost my hearing due to bacterial meningitis, and that's not even the saddest part about my life. As bad as that was I had parents who didn't want to bother raising what they claimed I was: a "broken" baby. To parents like mine, orphanages have always been a quick solution to their problems. Dump the kid—forget the kid. Well at least that's what my mother and father did when it came to me.

Silent moments transformed into silent days which transformed into silent years, and the many silent years brought isolation. So much isolation. At the beginning I was afraid of this unknown feeling, and then before I knew it, I was stuck in a world in between, which is not the best place to be. With time I gave up hoping that my parents would come back for me and no longer looked forward to daylight. Even though I lived with a sea of silent voices inside of me I also completely surrendered to the isolation. I gave up.

My parents never made the effort to come visit me at the orphanage. Fortunately, or most times, unfortunately, the rule in all the orphanages in Moldova is that children who have at least one parent are to be sent home during school breaks. Those were the only times I got to see my father and mother. Sadly, it became less important the more time I spent away from them. Mostly, I couldn't bear the fact that they couldn't be bothered to learn sign language in order to communicate with me. I felt like a broken stranger who came into their house a few times a year only to be reminded how much I wasn't wanted by them. At the end of every "vacation," I left for the orphanage a little more damaged inside than when I came.

When I was around the age of thirteen, my parents divorced. My father moved to Russia permanently and my mother remarried. Her husband was an alcoholic who never missed a chance to remind me that I was worthless. I don't know how it is in other parts of the world, but in Moldova, especially in villages, a deaf person is declared and believed to be stupid their entire life. My stepfather treated me no differently. He threw me out of the house countless times only because I wasn't "normal" and he was too embarrassed to be associated with a deaf child.

I started spending my school breaks at my grandmother's house. She was very ill. I worked hard and did my best to look after her so she wouldn't see me as a bother in her life. Grandma was as poor as my parents had been, so most days were a struggle for survival for the both of us.

By the time I aged out of the orphanage system, I managed to convince myself that I would never make it in the real world. I became the one that told herself that I wasn't smart enough, that I was too slow for the fast-paced world around me, and that I would never be able to achieve anything in life. During the last few days at the orphanage, I found myself staring at the bottom of the soup bowl wondering where my meals would come from once I was on the outside. Everything was so uncertain and so terrifying.

I tried. I got into a vocational school and started working to learn something that would hopefully keep me alive in the future. I slept in fear during the night, afraid of being raped by boys who thought I was too stupid to understand and too weak to defend myself. I starved during the days because I had no one to support me. My life became way worse than I could have imagined it.

Through the small deaf community in the city, I found out about The Orphan's Hands and the help they provide for those like me. I will forever be grateful to God for the opportunity to be part of this family. The Orphan's Hands rescued me from a life that I would like to forget at times. The work on yourself is the hardest, but also most important work in order to move forward. I hope with time I will stop asking why I was the one to become deaf and had to struggle in life. The difference between now and then is that because of The Orphan's Hands family I now understand that I was never broken, stupid, slow, or abnormal. My ears just didn't work—that's all.

Liviu

Some days you crave revenge. You dwell in it. You survive because of it. Growing up I thought having this feeling made me an awful person. Now I know it was something I felt because of my inability to stop my father from abusing my mother. It was the result of my helplessness in those moments.

I come from a family with eight siblings. My parents own a shed in the middle of the forest in a tiny village in Moldova. There was no electricity, no indoor plumbing, and no running water. Our family's income depended on whatever the forest had to offer with each season. Most times this meant going to bed hungry and being forced by my father to work harder the next day. The first memories I have are of myself in the forest collecting mushrooms, tea flowers and berries, or gathering firewood. Whatever my father didn't sell he kept for us to live on. There were countless nights when I would lie awake thinking if that was it. Was that all that life was about?

My childhood days were filled with endless chores and my father's non-stop abuse toward me, my siblings, and worst of all, my mother. There was nothing my father detested more than seeing us kids sitting around not doing anything. That's all it took for him to turn into someone we feared greatly. At times it felt like nothing in the world mattered to him except how many pounds of berries or tea flowers we brought home every night. He acted as if his children's whole purpose on earth was to labor non-stop.

One day, it was just another day: chores, yelling, and abuse. My mother, who was still recovering from my father's previous beating, was once again left by him lying on the floor crying. That was the day she left us. Today I understand that it must have taken real strength for her to get up and walk out of the house. That day, though, I was enraged. That night I went to sleep hoping I would wake up in the morning and my mother leaving us would have been just a nightmare.

My father woke us up very early the next morning, and that's when the real nightmare started. He began doubling the amount of work we had to do each day. He became even stricter and more abusive toward us. There were moments when I told myself that this was the life everyone around me was living and that if it was alright for everyone else I would have to accept it too. I started to realize that I didn't know any families in the village who didn't drink alcohol and no men that didn't abuse their wives daily. This is considered the norm where I come from.

I spent my time dreaming of the moment my mother would come back to us. But the day she did come home was the only day I wished she wouldn't have. It was that day that I felt so much, to the point where I stopped feeling anything at all except revenge. As soon as my father saw her, he dragged her into the house and locked all the doors behind him. I and my siblings stood in silence in front of our house. We were afraid to move, to speak, to run, to do anything to stop him. I stood there with my heart beating out of my chest and my legs shaking with weakness. But the moment I heard my mother's cry, I took off. My little hands began beating hard against the window. Part of me hoped it would make my father stop kicking her, but part of me was terrified to break the window, knowing he would get mad at me. I must have given up at some point because I remember the moment I turned around and saw all my brothers and sisters screaming, crying, and knocking on every window our house had. It was so bad that we all thought we would never get to see our mother alive again. She never ran away from home again.

Life became harder and our struggles got worse. Whatever the forest had to offer was no longer enough to keep us all alive. My parents' decision was to place me and my older siblings in the orphanage. That is how I ended up in the largest orphanage in the country of Moldova. Unlike most kids in that place, I was thankful to have ended up there. It wasn't because I had my own bed or because I had a meal three times a day. I was grateful for the fact that I no longer went to sleep at night plotting revenge against my father after watching him abuse my mother. At least I was far away from her helpless cries, and that somehow made it easier to breathe.

The teachers, however, never made it any easier for any kid in the orphanage. Every time I said something wrong or acted a little different than how I was supposed to, they would hint at me being this stupid by reminding me that I grew up in a forest. Compared to the life I lived back home, though, their hurtful words didn't do that much damage to me.

Every time I thought about the day when I would age out of the orphanage, my legs got weak and I felt sick. I was terrified of the idea that I would have to move back with my parents. That would be the end of my life, I thought.

Today, I am in a beautiful home surrounded by a huge family and am studying to become a doctor. The Orphan's Hands who saved my two older sisters from a life of hell and put them through school is now doing the same for me. They didn't just save my life; they also stopped me from becoming what my father is. If it wasn't for them I wouldn't have turned that constant craving of revenge into something that can help people today. I look forward to the day when

Liviu

my hands can help heal people, instead of hurt them like my dad did for so many years.

Tudor

I refused to let the darkness that surrounded me to corrupt my being. One of the many struggles that those of us born in ruins face, is staying good when everything around us is bad. I realized that I had two choices: kindness, which I believed would somehow make a way for me in life, and bitterness, which would just create another bad person just like my father. The choice became very simple.

Poverty, alcohol, and violence were part of my life since the beginning. My parents chose alcohol as an attempt to ignore the fact that they were poor. Quite soon violence became the result of my father's daily drinking. His brutality toward my mother broke me because I felt so small and helpless. I spent years being a silent witness to their endless fights. When my little sister, Ana, was born, she became my priority in life. I told myself that my purpose from then on was to protect her. Often, we went days without food and weeks without showering. School became a once in a while thing, and the hope that our parents would one day give us the care we needed was lost in despair.

There were times when running away from home was my and my sister's only way to survive. We wandered the streets dirty and hungry. I cannot begin to tell you how many times I wanted to give up during that kind of day. I felt so weary inside, so tempted to collapse under one of those blue-and-green wooden fences that surround most Moldovan houses, and never get up again. Instead, I kept walking. I faked my own courage so I could reassure my little sister that we would be alright. I knocked at many doors begging for help. Occasionally, a cousin of ours would take us in. For a few days, we had a warm meal and a bed to sleep in. She was kind in a world that was cruel.

The first time my mother left home my father got his revenge by beating me and Ana. "Where did she go?" he kept yelling at us. I consider the moment I gave up on trying to make sense of our life. I was no longer interested in trying to understand the reasons my parents had for being the way they were. My mother left me and Ana with this abusive monster, and there was no excuse for that.

Not long after, I found out my mother was now married to someone else and was living in the village nearby. I took my sister, and we walked all the way there, found her house, and knocked on her door. Thankfully she did not send us back to our father. My mother's new husband was just as poor as her ex-husband was. We constantly moved from one home to another. The winters were just as cold, and our bellies were just as empty as before.

I was thirteen years old when I was placed in the orphanage. Everyone around us kept telling my mother that this was the best choice she could make for us. Then, I wasn't so sure. Today, I am beyond thankful for ending up in an orphanage. If you had the life I had, you would understand why I believe that an orphanage is a better choice than "family."

It was there that I first heard about a loving God. To reach me He sent countless missionaries to what is, in our society, a forgotten, lonely place. The more I got to know Him, the more hope I had. After three years, I aged out of the orphanage, and instead of finding myself out on the streets like so many kids do every year, God sent very special people into my life. The Orphan's Hands took me in and cared for me and made me part of their family. I had endured a lot in my life because of cruel people, but

I was determined to focus on the few that showed me kindness. Kindness leads to love, and the world needs that, always.

Nicolae

I wish I could tell you the reason my parents abandoned me, but the truth is I simply don't know. I was four years old when they dropped me and my oldest brother off at an orphanage. I have never seen or heard from them again.

The twelve years that followed were spent hoping that someday they would come back for my brother and me. The fact that I didn't have a single photograph of them added to the pain. I was a lonely kid being haunted by two faceless figures. I needed them during the cold winter nights. I needed them when I was hungry. I needed them the first time I fell and scratched my knees. But most of all I needed them on my birthdays. I simply needed them. All I wanted was to know that I was good enough to be celebrated, that my life meant something to them.

I didn't have a great experience in the orphanage, but then I don't believe anyone ever does. It is a prison where those like me end up and are punished for our parents' mistakes. At sixteen years of age, I, like everyone else, aged out of the orphanage system. All I had to my name was a certificate of graduation and a document that labeled me as an orphan for the rest of my life.

Once I found myself on the street, I realized that the reality of my life had just gotten worse. The fact that I would have a bed to sleep in and three warm meals a day led me to a vocational school that was also considered a type of orphanage. The lack of determination during the next three years almost cost me my future. I believed that life wasn't fair to me and that I was owed something for everything I went through.

Thankfully, when I was at my lowest point, God put the Cameron family in my life. I was a lonely and angry boy who saw himself as a victim until the day I heard about the unconditional love of God. With the help of The Orphan's Hands I was admitted to a bible college and seminary, where I have been preparing to become a pastor. I went through a mess, and today I have a message. When you struggle in life, I encourage you to do the best you can to stop seeing yourself as a victim and start seeing yourself as a victor, because if I can do it, so can you.

Afterthought

You lie in your bed staring at the ceiling hoping that you fall asleep before everything inside you falls apart. You tell yourself that you don't have it as bad as those around you do. This thought temporarily takes away some of the weight you carry around daily.

The next morning you're up way too early to realize that the pain is still there. You make your bed with the same exactitude as the other dozen souls around you. You go on to complete the required morning chores and only slow down when you find yourself in front of a mirror while doing your morning hygiene. The trick is never to stare at yourself for too long, or you will definitely fall apart before you even begin your day. Before you

Afterthought

know it, it's 7:30 a.m. If you're lucky, breakfast is something worth eating that morning. Most days, though, it's so bad that you would rather leave the table as hungry as when you sat down.

At 8:00 a.m. you sit down at your desk and classes begin. Once in a while the teacher says something that interests you, which makes you snap out of whatever thought you had going through your mind at the time. It is as if your mind detaches from your body during classes. Your thoughts are all over the place, anywhere except there. During the few short breaks you have between classes, the "happy" kids go outside to run around. If you are part of the rest though, you spend it with your head on your desk, covered with a jacket feeling sorry for everything that isn't going right in your life.

When 2:30 p.m. finally comes, you walk with your class to the cafeteria hoping that lunch will be better than the breakfast you barely swallowed—or didn't. Somedays your shy self dares to ask for an extra piece of bread, which most likely gets you a shake of the head no. That leads to a few disgusted looks from those around you and a few minutes of embarrassment for even asking. The mentality in the orphanage is that it is something shameful to show how hungry you actually are and then ask for extra food. Even though every kid in that place is starving half the time.

The homework hours are from 4:00 p.m. until 6:30 p.m. You aren't allowed to speak during these hours unless it has to do with homework. As long as you sit quiet, you are alright. Well, that mostly depends on who your teacher is. Ours is the kind that takes this time to distribute the number of whips you "need" depending on the severity of your wrongdoing. He has a blue plastic gym stick, which he calls the blue pill that makes you better. It is kept in his office and brought to class whenever needed. Each misbehavior has a definite number of whips. You know if you miss a class how many you have to suffer through. If you get a bad grade, if you get into a fight, if you tell a lie, or if you are too noisy when you aren't supposed to. Some of these misbehaviors require so many whips that they are divided between days. To make matters worse, you are told to come in front of the classroom and bend forward toward the blackboard. The classroom is then asked if someone wants to do the whipping. In that moment only two things can happen: you are either whipped hard by someone you aren't getting along with, or you have family, like me, who volunteer to do it, hoping that theirs is a little less painful than the one from someone else. If the teacher doesn't like the severity of the one you get from a family member or friend, he then whips them to "teach" them how to do it right, and you get another one too. Let's just say it isn't fun to sit in your chair afterward.

Usually by dinner time at 7:30 p.m. you've given up on holding it together. You sit down at the table you share with five other kids and eat what's in front of you. Then, back at the dormitory, you finish your day the way you started it. Staring at yourself in the mirror while doing your nightly hygiene. Lights go off at 9:00 p.m., and that's when you begin telling yourself that maybe you don't have it as bad as others around you do. That's when your imagination becomes your anchor. You numb yourself by falling into this imaginary world full of imaginary things that are impossible. You never called it hope, because deep down you know the difference.

For those of you who have read this book, I wanted to give you a look into the daily routine of an orphanage. That is how I spent five years of my life, and that is how some of my friends spent fourteen years, twelve years, and nine years of their life.

Three states—I believe that when it came to us, there were three states of being. You either dissolved into your own suffering, constantly craved revenge, or were simply and purely numb. Your survival depended on in which one of these categories you were either born in or chose to be in. It

Afterthought

took me a long time to realize that I wouldn't be able to make it out alive with my back to the future and my eyes toward the past.

Forgiving, ignoring, accepting.

Going round and round in circles, punishing yourself every time you fall, and not rewarding yourself every time you get up.

Messed-up impressions about a life that shouldn't have been.

Fitting in a back piece without having a front piece.

... stories, stories, so many dark stories.

Merely lives that did not matter, pierced souls that did not burden.

Stencil days, infinite nights,

being content with nothing you had.

Portions of loneliness being poured over your head ... designing and plotting familiar escapes.

Things of this life dragged us to share, treasured moments cut from our shell.

What has had us broken, no longer intent, on destroying the thing that it once left for dead.

Facilities are crawling with stories like these, most not so lucky to get over it.

A duty entirely no longer exists,

to care for the others, for the least of these,

words that are used only when your eyes are covered in mist.

Dasa Rosca

Human Trafficking Statistics

Moldova: Tier-2 Watch List

As reported over the past five years, Moldova is primarily a source country for men, women, and children subjected to sex trafficking and forced labor. Moldovan victims are subjected to sex and labor trafficking within Moldova as well as in Russia, the Ukraine, and other countries in Europe, the Middle East, Africa, and East Asia. Women and children are subjected to sex trafficking in Moldova in brothels, saunas, and massage parlors. Increasingly, girls ages thirteen to fifteen are victims of sex trafficking. Child sex tourists, including from the EU, Turkey, Australia, Israel, Thailand, and the United States, subject Moldovan children to commercial sexual exploitation. The breakaway region of Transnistria remains a source for victims of both sex and labor trafficking. Official complicity in trafficking continues to be a significant problem in Moldova.[3]

The highest-ranking source countries for human trafficking—piling up human trafficking statistics daily—include Belarus, the **Republic of Moldova,** the Russian Federation, the **Ukraine,** Albania, Bulgaria, Lithuania, Romania, China, Thailand, and Nigeria.[4]

A human trafficker can receive up to 2,000 percent profit from a girl trafficked for sex.[5]

---

[3] "Trafficking in Persons Report June 2017," Department of State, accessed June 4, 2018.
https://www.state.gov/documents/organization/271339.pdf

[4] "Human Trafficking Statistics," Justice for Youth, accessed June 4, 2018. http://www.justiceforyouth.org/human-trafficking-statistics/

[5] "Human Trafficking Statistics," Justice for Youth.

Human Trafficking Statistics

The International Labor Organization estimates that there are **40.3 million** victims of human trafficking globally. [6]

- 81% of them are trapped in forced labor.
- 25% of them are children.
- 75% are women and girls.

The International Labor Organization estimates that forced labor and human trafficking is a **$150 billion** industry worldwide. [7]

The International Labor Organization estimates that there are **4.5 million people trapped in forced sexual exploitation globally.** [8]

In a 2014 report, the Urban Institute estimated that the underground sex

---

[6] "The Facts," The Polaris Project, accessed June 6, 2018. https://polarisproject.org/human-trafficking/facts

[7] "The Facts," The Polaris Project.

[8] "Sex Trafficking," The Polaris Project, accessed June 6, 2018. https://polarisproject.org/human-trafficking/sex-trafficking

economy ranged from **$39.9 million** in Denver, Colorado, to $290 **million** in Atlanta, Georgia.[9]

Every 30 Seconds another person becomes a victim of human trafficking.[10]

---

[9] "Sex Trafficking," The Polaris Project.

[10] "Human Trafficking—The Problem," Call to Freedom, accessed June 7, 2018. http://calltofreedom.org/human-trafficking/

What You Can Do

Make a donation. *Visit www.theorphanshands.org/donate to donate today.*

Pray for The Orphan's Hands. *Please pray for us as we pray for you. You can also send in your prayer requests.*

Start a gift drive. *We are always in need of new coats, boots, toys, nonperishable food items, and much more.*

Take a mission trip. *Change a life while you change your own! Visit Moldova and spend your days ministering to young men and women who have grown up being told they were worthless.*

Share this book with your friends and family. *Share these stories of redemption* *with your friends and family and help us tell their story.*

Invite The Orphan's Hands to come and share at your church. *We have a team of young men and women from Moldova traveling in the States for most of the year. We would love to share their stories with your organization. To schedule us, send us an email at contact@theorphanshands.org.*

Made in the USA
Columbia, SC
18 July 2018